FUN·TO·LEARN
COLOURS

Arianne Holden

Educational Consultant: Dr Naima Browne

LORENZ BOOKS

NOTES

Fun to Learn Colours introduces children to colours in lively and stimulating ways. The stunning and imaginative photographs show familiar objects that will encourage a child's eagerness to learn and to participate in the hands-on activities.

Learning the basics
Children need to be able to recognize colour and learn the names first of all. They should then be able to identify the colours of things around them. Later, the ideas of shades of colour and of mixing and matching colours are introduced.

Reading together
Most children benefit from adult help when reading a book for the first time. Do not expect a child to grasp all the information in the book in one go! Go through the book at the child's pace. This will ensure that reading times are always enjoyable.

Talking it through
Talk about the things you have found out together. Make everyday activities an adventure in learning. Getting dressed, preparing meals, tidying toys and all sorts of everyday activities provide opportunities to talk about colours and to broaden your child's understanding. For example, ask questions such as - What happens to my coffee when I add milk? Can you sort the blocks into sets of colours?

Answering questions
Encourage your child to answer questions. Don't worry if the answers are wrong – making mistakes is part of the learning process. The most important thing is that your child feels confident and willing to try. Remember, of course, to praise your child when he or she answers a question correctly.

Learning by doing
Encourage your child to try all the activities. They have been specially designed to be easy and fun to do, and little preparation is required.

CONTENTS

Red

Red is the colour of ripe tomatoes and soft, sweet strawberries.

shades of red

big red hair scrunch

What will happen to this tomato?

spicy red chillies

up ...

up and down on the red see-saw

three scuttling red crabs

... and dow

Who's going to eat the juicy, red strawberries?

Did you know?

When you're shy or angry, your cheeks can turn red! Has this ever happened to you?

Green

Green is the colour of crisp, crunchy apples and grass.

shades of green

I'm hiding in the long, green grass.

Which green things am I made from?

Hop to it, hoppity green frog!

Green cactus spines are prickly.

oUCH!

Try this!

Cress creature

1. Put damp cotton wool into an egg cup.

2. Scatter cress seeds and water every day.

3. Watch the cress grow.

4. Paint a face on the egg cup. Look at all that green hair!

5

Blue

Blue is the colour of the sea and sky on a sunny day. Is the sky blue today?

shades of blue

two blue slithery snakes

Hisss!

blue cap with blue bobbles

Ted's favourite colour is blue.

How many blue whales can you count?

watch out!

three dancing blue aliens

There's a blue frisbee about!

Do you think I can knock down the blue skittles? Can you play skittles?

Orange

Orange is a happy colour.
It is the colour of crunchy
carrots and juicy oranges.

shades of orange

Rabbits
love carrots.

Try this!

Make frozen orange juice

1. Wash a small pot.

2. Trace the top of the pot.

3. Cut it out and make a slit.

4. Fill the pot with juice and top with the card. Push a lolly stick into the slit and freeze. When frozen, lift off the pot.

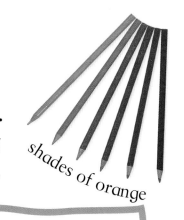

orange socks

orange trousers

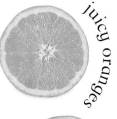

juicy oranges

orange flowers

bright orange hat and bright orange t-shirt

Where did I put my orange?

Do you like eating carrots?

Yellow

Yellow is the colour of sour lemons and sweet bananas.

shades of yellow

How many yellow bananas has this monkey eaten?

quack ...

quack ...

quack ...

bright yellow ducks

a shower of yellow daisies

disco dancing yellow corn on the cob

Try this!

Sunshine biscuits

1. Mix icing sugar, lemon juice and yellow food colouring in a bowl.

2. Spread icing on to some biscuits.

3. Can you taste the lemon? Is it sweet or sour?

Purple

Purple is the colour of big, juicy grapes and smooth, shiny aubergines.

shades of purple

noisy purple shakers

One …

two …

…three purple snails.

purple flowers tied with purple ribbon

fluttering purple butterflies

purple recorder

purple grapes

How many aubergines can the chef juggle?

Brown

Brown is the colour of cuddly puppies, chewy toffee and muddy footprints.

shades of brown

one

two

three brown pine cones

Wombat's wobbly tower of brown pine cones.

a litter of brown puppies

cuddly brown Ted's cartwheeling extravaganza

muddy brown footprints

Soft, brown feathers feel ticklish.

chewy brown toffee and chocolate

Pink

Pink is the colour
of soft, sweet
marshmallows
and your fingernails.

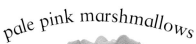
shades of pink

What colour is your tongue?

pale pink marshmallows

bright pink bowl

rosy pink bear

Save some creamy, pink pudding for me!

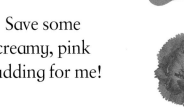

Try this!

Making pink dye

1. Put two beetroots in warm water. Leave till the water is pink.

2. Remove them. Place an old white t-shirt in the water. Soak overnight.

I'm dressed in pink from head to toe.

3. Take the t-shirt out of the bowl. What colour is it?

11

Black

You see black when you close your eyes.

What colour are these things?

A juicy black fly for a hungry black spider.

black bat mask

cool black sunglasses

Can you count ten black fingers?

Giddy-up, black ponies!

Where are these shiny black beetles going?

black sheriff's hat

black bowler hat

White

White is the colour of snow on a cold winter's day and fluffy clouds on a summer's day.

Can you find any white things?

fluffy white kitten

one

two

three

frisky white lambs

Doctor Rosie will make the polar bear better.

wibbly wobbly snowman

Try this!

Make meringue snow cakes

2. Spoon cream into each meringue.

1. Whisk up some cream in a bowl.

creamy white ice cream

Gold

Gold is a colour that glistens like shining stars and royal crowns.

gold glitter, thread and crayons

three gold rings

two gold bangles

glitzy gold wig

Look at Pirate Ted's sparkling gold treasure.

Try this!

Make a gold crown

1. Draw a crown shape on to card. Cut it out.

2. Glue gold foil on to your crown.

3. Join the ends with sticky tape.

I'm catching falling stars.

I've won a gold medal!

Silver

Silver is a shiny colour. Sometimes you can see your reflection in things that are silver.

silver crayons, glitter and thread

shiny, silver spaceship

toot!
toot!
toot!

What colour are Ted's weights?

Astronaut Teds wear silver spacesuits and helmets.

brr

silver alarm clock

Look at my silver fancy dress!

ticklish, silver tinsel scarf

Bronze

Bronze is a shiny colour. It looks a little like gold.

bronze thread and crayons

flickering bronze mirror ball

three wild, wiry bronze men

marvellous magician in a bronze cloak and hat

abracadabra!

Vroooom!

brilliant bronze racing cars

one

two

three

glowing bronze bow

cool bronze sunglasses

I'm a bronze robot.

dazzling bronze crown

Rainbow

There are seven colours in a rainbow. Do you know what they are called?

red
orange
yellow
green
blue
indigo
violet

Ted is painting a rainbow just for you.

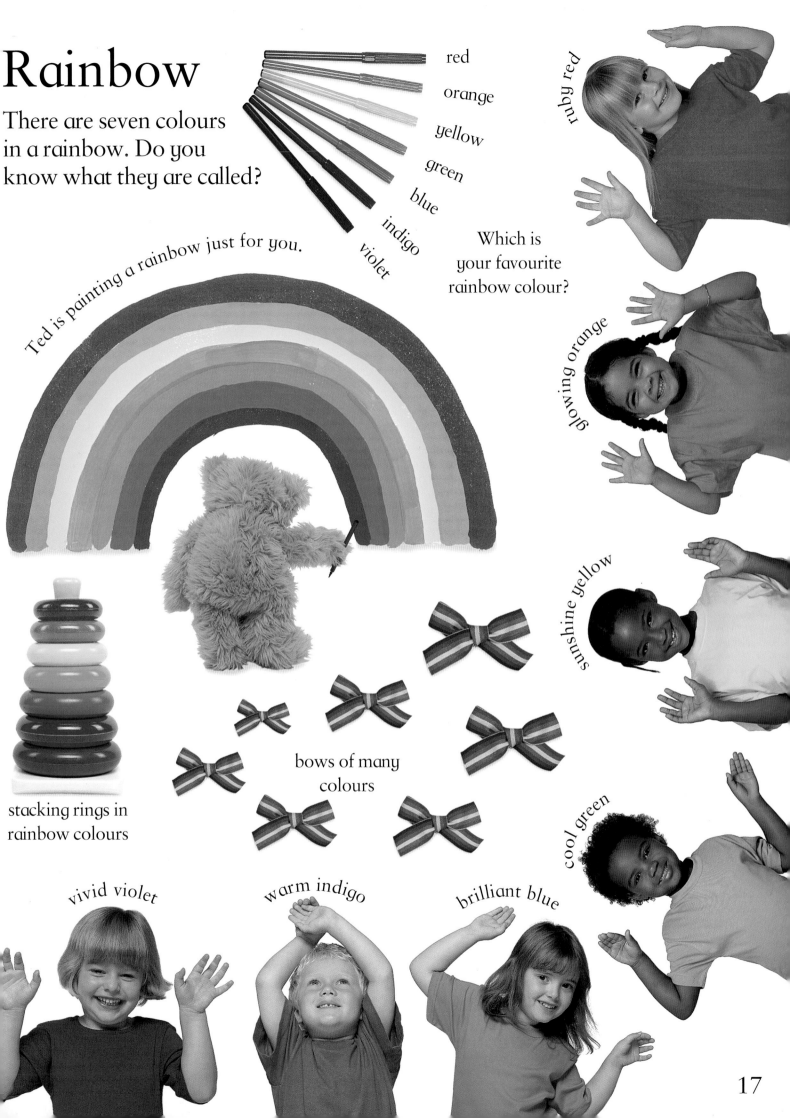

Which is your favourite rainbow colour?

ruby red

glowing orange

sunshine yellow

cool green

stacking rings in rainbow colours

bows of many colours

vivid violet

warm indigo

brilliant blue

Dark to light

Colours can be different shades. Some are light shades and some are dark. Can you see the colours getting lighter?

dark blue

Dangling blue ribbons ..

dark red

Ted's red paper hat ..

dark green

A smart green bow tie ..

dark yellow

Pretty yellow petals ..

light blue

... get lighter and lighter and even lighter.

light red

... gets lighter and lighter and even lighter.

light green

... gets lighter and lighter and even lighter.

light yellow

.. get lighter and lighter and even lighter.

19

Light to dark

These pictures show some colours getting darker and darker. Run a finger along the lines of colours from light to dark.

light pink

The pink butterflies ..

light brown

The slithery brown snail's shell ..

light purple

The alien's long hair ...

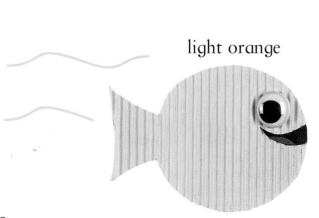

light orange

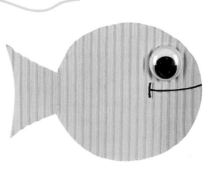

The splishy, splashy fish ...

20

dark pink

dark brown

... get darker and darker and darker.

... gets darker and darker and even darker.

dark purple

... gets darker and darker and even darker.

dark orange

... get darker and darker and even darker.

21

Mixing colours

When you mix colours, you make new colours. If you have red, blue and yellow paints, you can make all the colours of the rainbow!

red

blue   yellow

Blue monster is ready to get mixing!

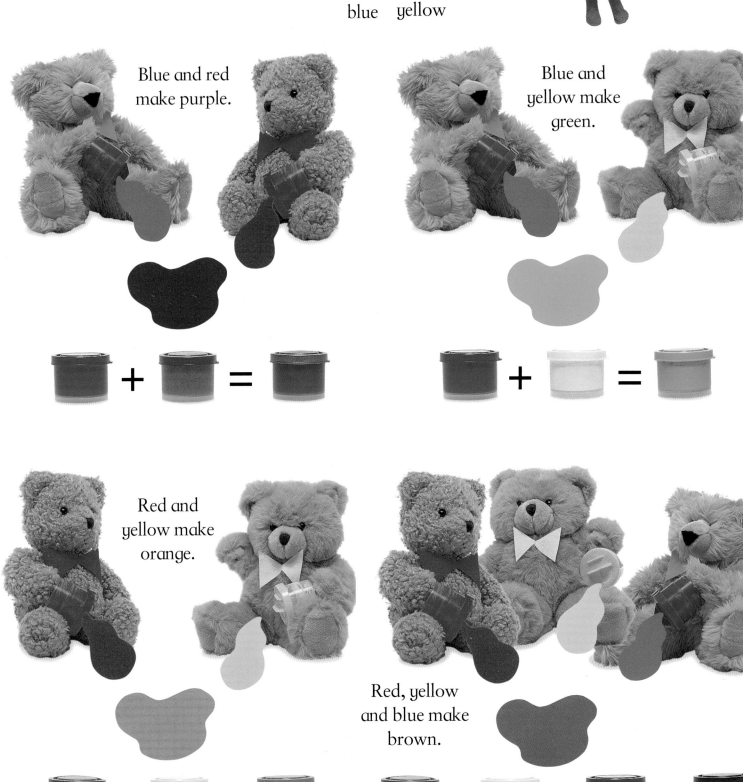

Blue and red make purple.

Blue and yellow make green.

Red and yellow make orange.

Red, yellow and blue make brown.

How do you make ...

... orange?

... purple?

... green?

... brown?

Try this!

Mixing colours

1. You will need red, blue and yellow paints, a paintbrush and a pot of water.

2. Mix the colours to make brown, green, orange and purple.

3. Use the colours to paint

a brown teddy

a bright green pear

an orange stripey cat

a bunch of purple grapes

Making light colours

Make a paint colour lighter by mixing white into it. A light colour is sometimes called a pale colour.

Blue monster loves mixing light colours.

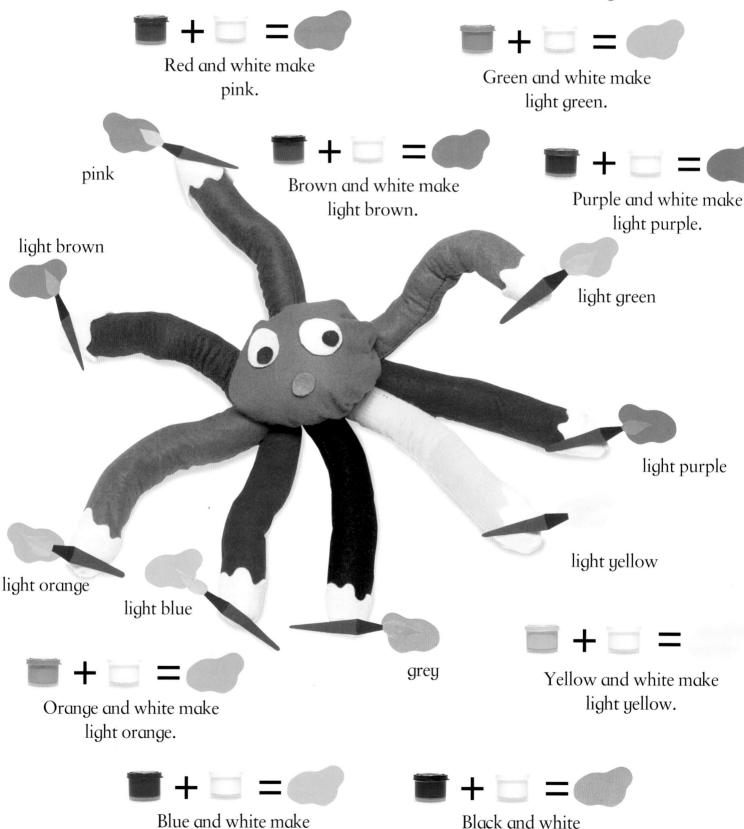

+ = Red and white make pink.

+ = Green and white make light green.

+ = Brown and white make light brown.

+ = Purple and white make light purple.

pink

light brown

light green

light purple

light yellow

light orange

light blue

grey

+ = Orange and white make light orange.

+ = Yellow and white make light yellow.

+ = Blue and white make light blue.

+ = Black and white make grey.

24

Try this!

Making light colours

1. You will need red, yellow, blue and white paint, a paintbrush and a pot of water.

2. Choose a colour paint and mix it with white.

3. Make light colours to paint

a grey elephant

a pale blue bird

a pink fluffy bunny

a light green bug

Which light and dark colours can you find at home?

dark pink and light pink shoes

dark purple

light purple

red legs

A light blue t-shirt ...

... and a dark blue t-shirt.

dark red legs.

25

Colours in nature

The natural world is full of wonderful colours. Sometimes things in nature change colour.

Leaves are green in summer, but ...

... gold and brown in autumn.

Grapes can be green or purple.

Young fir cones are green.

Apples can be different colours.

green apple

red and green apple

Older cones are brown.

red apple

Bees collect nectar from colourful flowers.

Sunlight reflects off the golden beetle and dazzles its enemies.

Flamingos are pink when they eat pink shrimps.

Male ducks are colourful. Can you point to the male duck?

The marbled gecko changes the colour of its skin to match its hiding place.

The three-toed sloth is green because a tiny plant grows in its fur. It does not hurt the sloth.

The chameleon is camouflaged to match the branch.

27

Favourite colours

The children have chosen their favourite colours. Which colour do you like most of all?

Astronaut Ted likes silver because it's shiny.

I like all the colours of the rainbow.

Purple is perfect for my puppet.

Yellow makes me happy.

My monster and I like blu

I like red. Strawberries are red.

Chocolate-brown is my favourite colour.

My cuddly frog is green.

White is
right for me.

I like
orange most
of all!

My best
dance outfit
is black.

Glistening gold is my favourite.

Bronze is my
ourite colour. My
crown is bronze.

Can you guess what
colour I like?

29

Treasure hunt

Choose red, green, blue or yellow. Then find, make or draw all the things pictured along the matching coloured line. You can play this alone or with friends.

START HERE

Find, make or draw these red things.

beads

t-shirt

cherry-red cherries

Find, make or draw these green things.

cuddly toy

beetle picture

prickly cactus

Find, make or draw these blue things.

felt tip pens

cuddly toy

seaside picture

Find, make or draw these yellow things.

pretty flowers

number two

hat

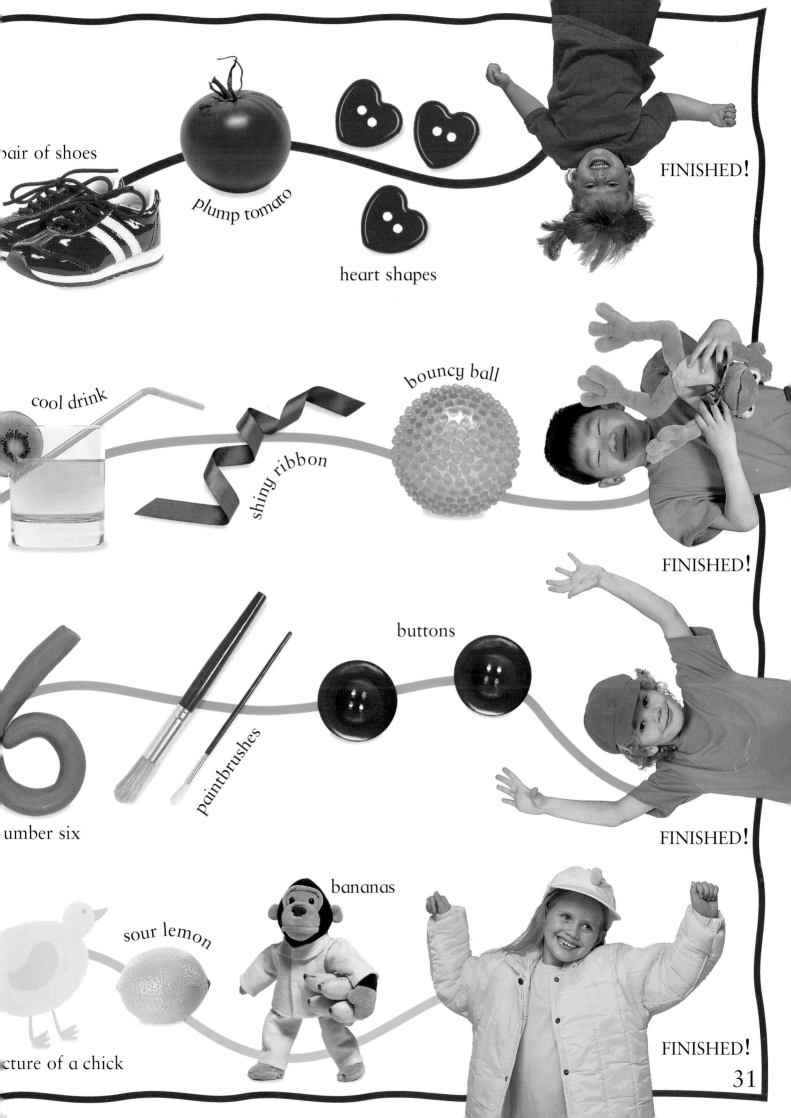

pair of shoes

plump tomato

heart shapes

FINISHED!

cool drink

bouncy ball

shiny ribbon

FINISHED!

buttons

paintbrushes

umber six

FINISHED!

bananas

sour lemon

cture of a chick

FINISHED!

First published in 1998 by Lorenz Books

© Anness Publishing Limited 1998

Lorenz Books is an imprint of Anness Publishing Limited
Hermes House, 88-89 Blackfriars Road, London SE1 8HA

This edition distributed in Canada by Raincoast Books, 8680 Cambie Street,
Vancouver, British Columbia V6P 6M9

ISBN 1 85967 680 4

A CIP catalogue record for this book is available from the British Library

Publisher: Joanna Lorenz
Managing Editor, Children's Books: Sue Grabham
Project Manager: Lyn Coutts
Consultant: Dr Naima Browne, Department of Education, University of London
Reader: Penelope Goodare
Design: Mike Leaman Design Partners
Photography: John Freeman
Head Stylist: Melanie Williams
Stylist: Ken Campbell
Production Controller: Ben Worley

The Publishers would like to thank the following children for modelling for this book:
Rosie Anness, Daisy Bartlett, Ambika Berczuk, Andrew Brown, April Cain, Callum
Collins, Rubin Fox, Africa George, Safari George, Saffron George, Madison
Harrington, Faye Harrison, Carolina Martin de Silver, Rebekah Murrell, Lucie Ozanne
Martin, Philip Quach, Tom Rawlings, Alfie Smeton, Georgina Thomas.

Picture Credits: 27tl, 27c, 27bl © Bruce Coleman Limited; 27tr, 27tc © Natural
Science Photos; 27br © Planet Earth Pictures.

Printed in Hong Kong/China

1 3 5 7 9 10 8 6 4 2